Sanskrit is Fun

PART II

*The Editors wish to acknowledge the role played by David Stollar
and other members of the St James School Sanskrit faculty
in the preparation of the material for the Sanskrit Course.*

Sanskrit is Fun

A Sanskrit Coursebook For Beginners

Edited by
WARWICK JESSUP
ELENA JESSUP

PART II

MOTILAL BANARSIDASS PUBLISHERS
PRIVATE LIMITED ● DELHI

First Indian Edition : Delhi, **2012**
First Edition: London, 2005

Published under arrangements with
St. James School,
Sanskrit Department, London

ISBN : 978-81-208-3545-0 (PB Part I)
978-81-208-3546-7 (PB Part II)
978-81-208-3547-4 (PB Part III)

MOTILAL BANARSIDASS
41 U.A. Bungalow Road, Jawahar Nagar, Delhi 110 007
8 Mahalaxmi Chamber, 22 Bhulabhai Desai Road, Mumbai 400 026
203 Royapettah High Road, Mylapore, Chennai 600 004
236, 9th Main III Block, Jayanagar, Bengaluru 560 011
Sanas Plaza, 1302 Baji Rao Road, Pune 411 002
8 Camac Street, Kolkata 700 017
Ashok Rajpath, Patna 800 004
Chowk, Varanasi 221 001

Printed using Times, Marking-RomanTM (transliteration) and
SanskritpadaTM fonts designed and distributed by
6H Software, London (Tel. 020-8944 9496); © 1993-4 6H Software.

COVER DRAWING: Giraffe with Sanskrit lettering

Printed in India
By Jainendra Prakash Jain at Shri Jainendra Press,
A-44, Naraina, Phase-I, New Delhi 110 028
and published by Narendra Prakash Jain for
Motilal Banarsidass Publishers Private Limited,
Bungalow Road, Delhi 110 007

Foreword

by Prof Dr Satya Vrat Shastri

After a thorough perusal of these text books written by teachers of St James Schools in London for the teaching of Sanskrit, I am convinced of their utility for Indian schools. They are well-graded and supported by appropriate illustrations that make them very attractive to learners, particularly the young.

Today many Indian universities offer Sanskrit as an optional subject, even for those who are majoring in other subjects. For these students the books would be very effective in introducing them to Sanskrit which they might not have studied previously. The books could also be useful for those involved in performing arts like dance and music, or for students of Yoga and Ayurveda, subjects which have many Sanskrit references.

The first group of books entitled Sanskrit is Fun (3 volumes) introduce the learners to the Devanagari alphabet grouping the letters according to their place of articulation. Each group is given a designation, 'Family'. The 'Family' comprises both the vowels and the consonants. The learners are first taught how to draw the letters. The teaching is also helped by the humorous presentation of them in the form of animal figures. The next step is to add vowels to the consonants and then to teach joint consonants. Finally words and sentences are formed.

The second group of books seek to teach Sanskrit with reference to age-old stories of Krishna (2 volumes) and Rama (2 volumes). These stories with perennial interest of their own are then pressed into service to teach vocabulary, the formation of nouns and the conjugation of verbs in all three tenses. Adjectives and prepositions are also covered .

By the time learners have completed these books it is expected they would have a good basic grasp of the Sanskrit language, its vocabulary, structure and grammar. These books are an attempt to teach Sanskrit in a simple and systematic way that may well dispel the notion that Sanskrit is a difficult language.

Dr Shastri is currently an Honorary Professor at the Special Centre for Sanskrit Studies, Jawaharlal Nehru University, New Delhi. He was the Head of the Department of Sanskrit and the Dean of the Faculty of Arts at the University of Delhi, where he was the Pandit Manmohan Nath Dar Professor of Sanskrit (1970–1995).

Preface

by Professor Richard Gombrich

It is a privilege for me to be invited to introduce this set of textbooks. They have been compiled with loving care by the teachers of the Sanskrit Department of St James School in London. Their slow birth reflects the years of teaching experience which have gone into their making.

Sanskrit is by no means an easy language: even in India it is mastered only by a small minority of the population. The grammar is complicated, even if someone who masters it will finally discover that it is more systematic and less irregular than that of English. The vocabulary is vast, reflecting the vast span of time and geographical area over which Sanskrit has been used. Learning to read and write an Indian script is also a major undertaking for a student from another culture. (Luckily for us Europeans, at least it is written left to write and top to bottom.)

On the other hand, Sanskrit is not only a beautiful language written in a beautiful script; it is the vehicle of classical Indian culture, the culture which has given the world one of its greatest literatures and greatest civilizations. Sanskrit achieved something not very different from the form it still has today more than three thousand years ago. The reason why it has survived so well, and may well outlive most of the languages which the world is now using, is not hard to understand: it is because of the aesthetic attractions and the intellectual and spiritual value of the content of so many Sanskrit texts.

Only a few students are likely to have the opportunity to go on to study Sanskrit in depth, so that they can enjoy reading Sanskrit by themselves. There will be so many rival claims on their attention. But even those who only work through these books are likely to look back on the experience with satisfaction, a feeling that they have done something truly worth while. And the few who go further will be grateful that these books have launched them on an unforgettable experience.

Prof Gombrich was the Boden Professor of Sanskrit at the University of Oxford from 1976 to 2004 and was a past President of the Pali Text Society (1994–2002) and General Editor Emeritus of the Clay Sanskrit Library. He is currently the Boden Professor of Sanskrit Emeritus, University of Oxford

NOTES FOR TEACHERS AND STUDENTS

Part Two: Joining Vowels to Consonants

Ideally, the students should see the writing of the letter demonstrated and then copy it , perhaps one part at a time, depending on how complicated it is.

In general, the order for writing each letter is as follows:
- *(a) the top line is drawn first,*
- *(b) then the descender,*
- *(c) then any additional shape, and*
- *(d) finally the vowel.*

When writing a letter, the student should hear the sound in mind. Each time the student hears the sound of the letter in mind while writing it, the connection between sound and shape is reinforced.

The students should always be encouraged to write each character more perfectly than the one before. This ensures that the writing improves rather than deteriorates.

It is worth mentioning that both traditionally and in the best modern practice the top line of each letter is written first and, even when writing words, only enough of this line is written for one letter at a time.

READING PRACTICE

Daily reading charts are given at regular intervals during the course to provide the necessary practice. These should be read every day until another reading chart is given in the text. This practice is only effective if the teacher ensures that each student's finger is exactly beneath the letter being read. When the students can read a page fluently they should be asked to read it backwards (i.e., moving from right to left).

DAILY AND WEEKLY TESTING

No written course can act as a substitute for a teacher's or student's intelligence and ingenuity. Ideally, each step would be measured precisely to the needs of each pupil. Tests need to be given to ensure that the student is ready for the next stage.   The following should be practised regularly:

- *(a) reading of letters and words written in a random order on the blackboard (or, in the case of a student, on paper), and*

(b) *dictation: a weekly dictation of the letters covered that week and in previous weeks. This stimulates the student's interest in learning and acts as a guide for the teacher as to the effectiveness of the teaching.*

THE WRITING OF SANSKRIT

Each Sanskrit letter is a 'character' and can be appreciated best in the initial stages by writing without reliance on any guidelines on the page. After a little while a top line is useful from which to hang the letters. Each letter should be hung freely from this line without attempting to touch a bottom line. In this respect, it is comparable to English writing, where the letters rest on the bottom line and there is no attempt to touch the top line. Thus, in Sanskrit, there will always be a space between the bottom of the letters and the next line down.

There is another factor to note in the writing of Sanskrit letters. Calligraphy has traditionally been done on a slanting surface, and this is recommended for the writing of Sanskrit. One reason for this is that the student's back is thereby allowed to be more upright and there is a closer view of the writing, encouraging finer attention.

When a vowel is added to a consonant, the writing should follow the order of the sound, i.e., consonant first, then the vowel.

SANSKRIT RECITATION

As was noted for the previous part of this course, during the learning of any language, whilst the elements of that language are being introduced, it is helpful if examples of Sanskrit literature are recited on a daily basis. This gives a taste of the beauty of the language.

Daily Reading Chart 7

अ क ख ग च ङ ह

इ च छ ज भ ञ य श

ऋ ट ठ ड ढ ण र ष

ऌ त थ द ध न ल स

उ प फ ब भ म व

Revision of the Five Families

Read and copy each family beautifully. Then see if you can write out each family from memory in your exercise book. No cheating!

अ	क	ख	ग	च	ङ	ह

इ	च	छ	ज	झ	ञ	य	श

ऋ	ट	ठ	ड	ढ	ण	र	ष

ल	त	य	द	ध	न	ल	स

उ	प	फ	ब	भ	म	व

Consonants with इ

Sound and copy the following:

क	....	कि	....
त	....	ति	....
प	....	पि	....
म	....	मि	....
स	....	सि	....

Now you add an ड़ to the following letters.
The first one is done for you.

क

ब

न

ल

ज

द

र

च

Consonants with उ

Sound and copy the following:

क	....	कु	....
म	....	मु	....
ज	....	जु	....
ग	....	गु	....
स	....	सु	....

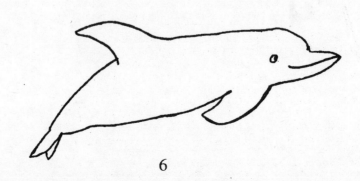

Now you add an उ to the following letters.
The first one is done for you.

क	कु
व	
ल	
च	
ठ	
ह	
न	
ष	

Add an इ and an उ to the following letters.
The first one is done for you.

क ग ब ल प न

कि कु

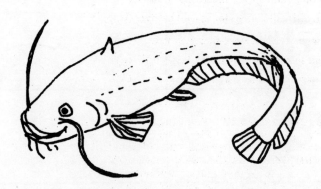

Consonants with ऋ

Sound and copy the following:

क	....	कृ	....
त	....	तृ	....
म	....	मृ	....
ग	....	गृ	....
प	....	पृ	....

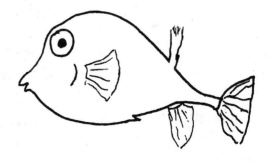

9

Now you add a ऋ to the following letters.
The first one is done for you.

क	कृ
ज	
श	
द	
न	
ब	
म	
व	

Add an इ, an उ, and a ऋ to the following letters. The first one is done for you.

क कि कु कृ

ग _____ _____ _____

ब _____ _____ _____

श _____ _____ _____

प _____ _____ _____

न _____ _____ _____

11

Consonants with
Vowels

Now sound and write the following:

क	कि	कु	कृ

त	ति	तु	तृ

Consonants with
Vowels

Can you read the following?

क	कि	कु	कृ
त	ति	तु	तृ
म	मि	मु	मृ
प	पि	पु	पृ
ज	जि	जु	जृ
म	मि	सु	सृ

Consonants with Vowels

Sound and copy the following, or you may
be eaten by the shark!

ग				न			
गि				नि			
गु				नु			
गृ				नृ			

Consonants with Vowels

Sound and copy these letters. Now see if you can write them all from memory in your exercise book.

क	कि	कु	कृ

15

Read the swans.

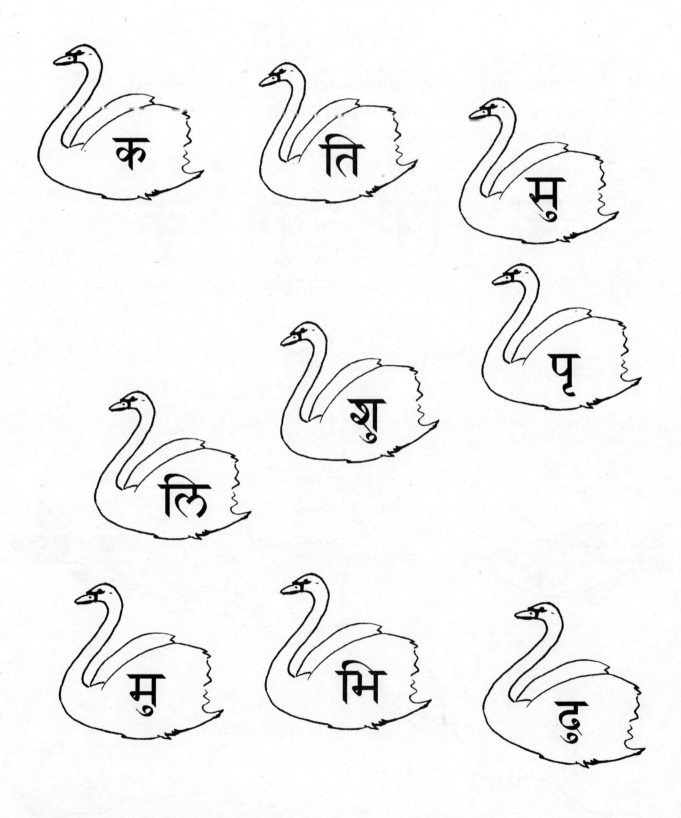

Reading Practice

Read the following across. When you see two dots (:) after a word, this means breathe out.   This is called a visarga.

अ	अप	अपि	
अ	अम	अमि	
इ	इत	इति	
प	पु	पुन	पुनः
त	तु		
क	कु	कुत	कुतः
म	मृ	मृग	मृगः
म	मृ	मृत	

Reading and Writing Practice

Read the following words and then copy them:

अपि	....
अमि	....
इति	....
पुनः	....
तु	....
कुतः	....
मृगः	....
मृत	....

Revision of
Five Families

Read and copy each family.

अ		इ		ऋ		ऌ		उ	
क		च		ट		त		प	
ख		छ		ठ		य		फ	
ग		ज		ड		द		ब	
घ		झ		ढ		ध		भ	
ङ		ञ		ण		न		म	
ह		य		र		ल		व	
		श		ष		स			

Long and Short Vowels

Sound and copy each letter:

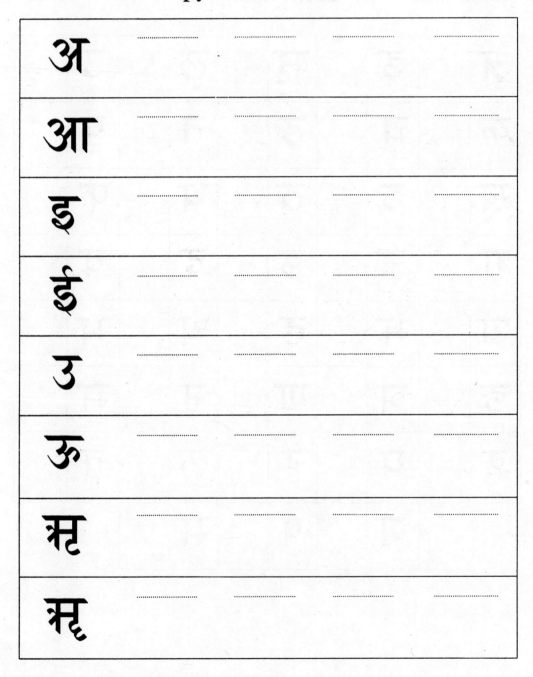

अ	⋯⋯	⋯⋯	⋯⋯
आ	⋯⋯	⋯⋯	⋯⋯
इ	⋯⋯	⋯⋯	⋯⋯
ई	⋯⋯	⋯⋯	⋯⋯
उ	⋯⋯	⋯⋯	⋯⋯
ऊ	⋯⋯	⋯⋯	⋯⋯
ऋ	⋯⋯	⋯⋯	⋯⋯
ॠ	⋯⋯	⋯⋯	⋯⋯

Daily Reading Chart 8

अ आ इ ई उ ऊ ऋ ॠ ऌ

अ क ख ग च ङ ह

इ च छ ज झ ञ य श

ऋ ट ठ ड ढ ण र ष

ऌ त थ द ध न ल स

उ प फ ब भ म व

Apples and Pears

Each apple and pear is missing its long or short vowel. Can you fill them in?

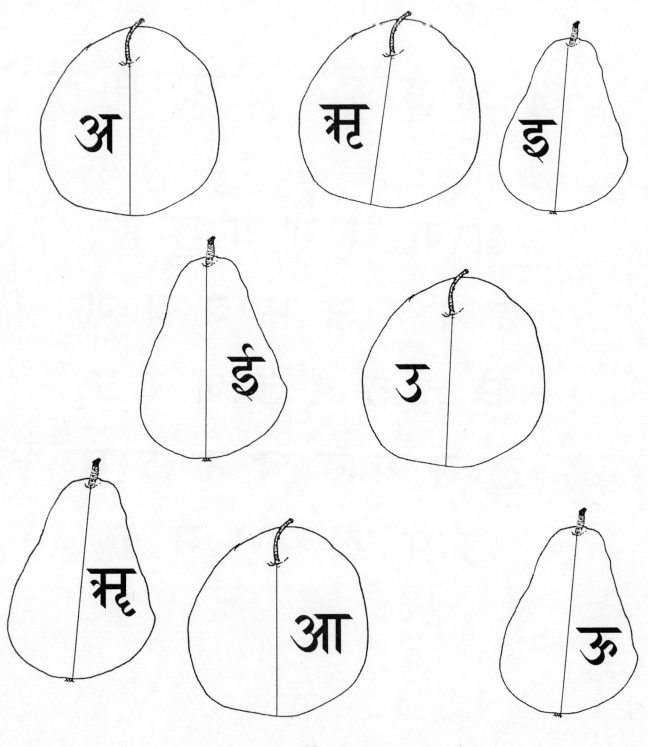

The Snake

Can you read the letters that this snake has just had for dinner?

Alphabet Revision Game

Read the letters on the fish. Then, draw a line around fish in the same family. The अ family is done for you.

A letter with an आ has an extra line.
Sound and copy the following:

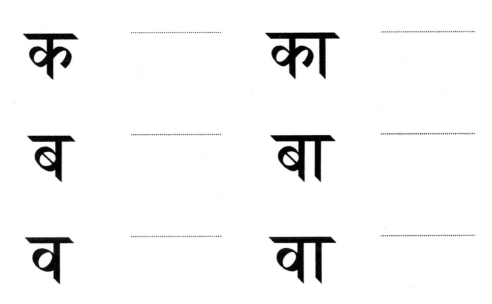

क

का

ब

बा

व

वा

Now you add an आ to the following letters:

त

ला

ल

न

ह

A letter with an ई has a loop going forward.
Sound and copy the following:

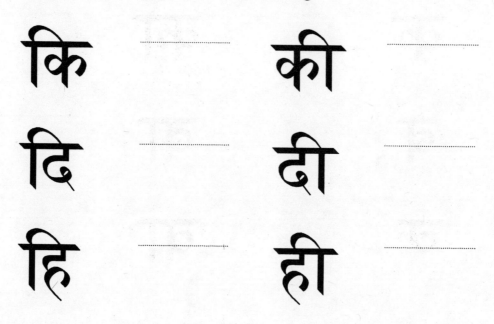

कि .... की ....

दि .... दी ....

हि .... ही ....

Now you add an ई to the following letters:

त   ︵ली︶

ल   ....

न   ....

ब   ....

Add an आ, an इ, and an ई to the following
letters. The first one is done for you.

क	का	कि	की
त			
ग			
ष			
प			
ण			

A letter with a long आ has a tadpole lying on its face, not on its back.

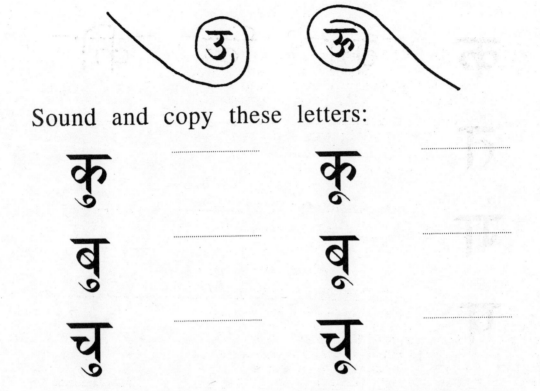

Sound and copy these letters:

कु .... कू ....

बु .... बू ....

चु .... चू ....

Now you add an ऊ to the following letters:

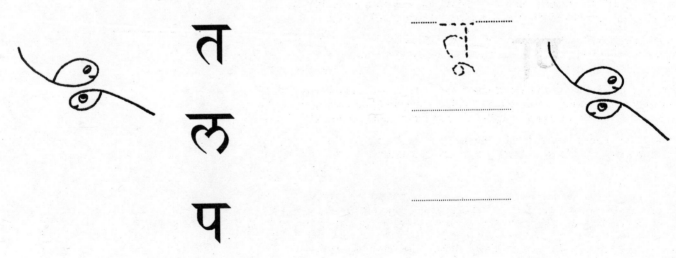

त

ल

प

Add an आ, an इ, an ई, an उ, and an ऊ to the following letters.   The first line is done for you.

क	का	कि	की	कु	कू
ह					
ङ					
च					
ड					
व					

A ऋ has two hooks, not just one.

Sound and copy the folowing:

कृ   कृ

जृ   जृ

नृ   नृ

Now you add a ऋ to the following letters:

त   तृ

म

व

म

Add an आ, an इ, an ई, an उ, an ऊ, a ऋ and a ॠ
to the following letters.   The first one is
done for you.

त	ता	ति	ती	तु	तू	तृ	तॄ
क							
म							
श							

Consonants with Long and Short Vowels

Sound and write:

क	का	कि	की
....	....	....	....
....	....	....	....
....	....	....	....

Sound and write:

कु	कू	कृ	कॄ
....	....	....	....
....	....	....	....
....	....	....	....

Go up the stairs.

The Cloudy Day Puzzle

Fill in the missing letters in the clouds. Look at the ones filled in to see how to do it.

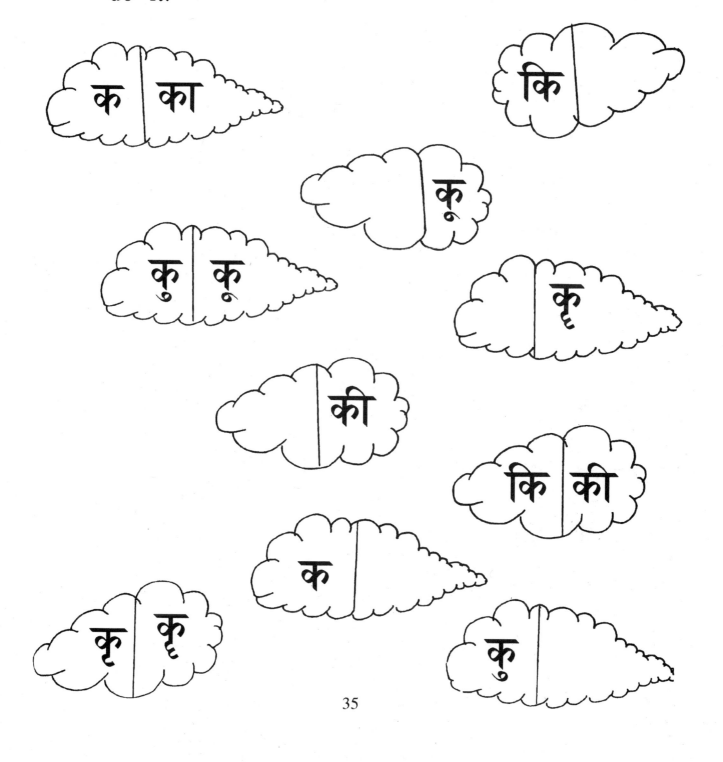

Now we can write all the vowels with any letter. Sound and write the columns going downward.

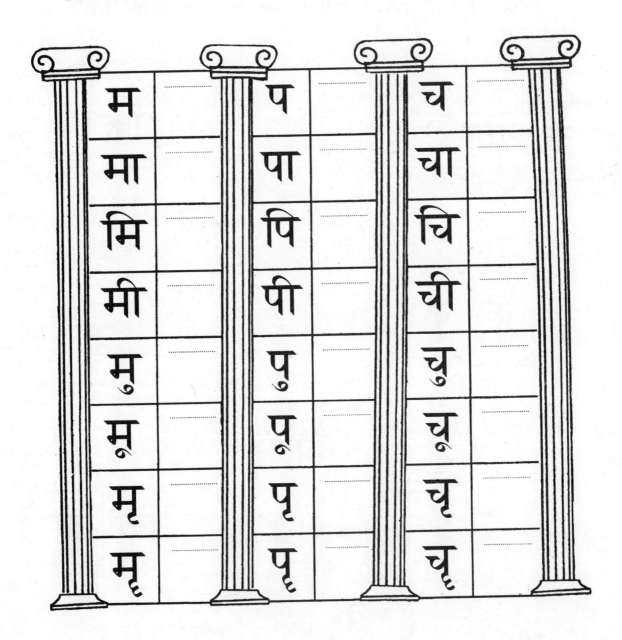

म		प		च	
मा		पा		चा	
मि		पि		चि	
मी		पी		ची	
मु		पु		चु	
मू		पू		चू	
मृ		पृ		चृ	
मॄ		पॄ		चॄ	

Mount Sanskrit

Can you reach the flag at the top of the mountain? Read all the letters to find the route to the top. Then read your way back to base camp.

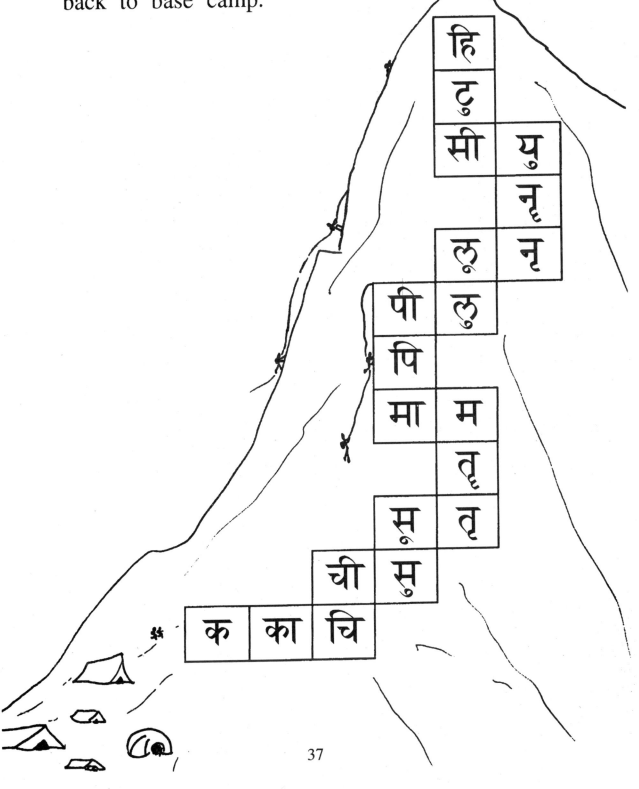

Revision of
Five Families

Read and copy each family.
They are in a backwards order!

ह		श		ष		म			
ङ		य		र		ल		व	
च		ञ		ण		न		म	
ग		झ		ढ		ध		भ	
ख		ज		ड		द		ब	
क		छ		ठ		थ		फ	
अ		च		ट		त		प	
		इ		ॠ		ळ		उ	

✸ ✸ ✸ ✸ ✸ ✸ ✸ ✸ ✸ ✸

Consonants and Vowels

Sound and copy.

ज	जा	जि	जी	जु	जू	जृ	जॄ
ग	गा	गि	गी	गु	गू	गृ	गॄ
त	ता	ति	ती	तु	तू	तृ	तॄ

Now, add long and short vowels to the letter क. Write them in the order shown above.

क	....	....	....	....	....	....	....

The Smiling Snail

Keep the snail happy by filling in his shell correctly.   Can you follow the pattern?

Start from the middle of the snail.   Some letters have already been written.

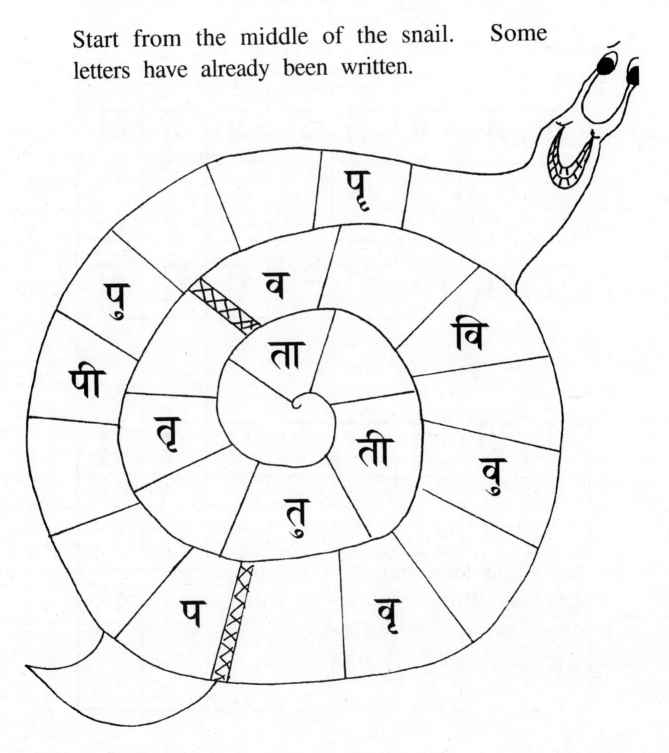

Help the Children Get to School

Read these correctly to help the children get to school:

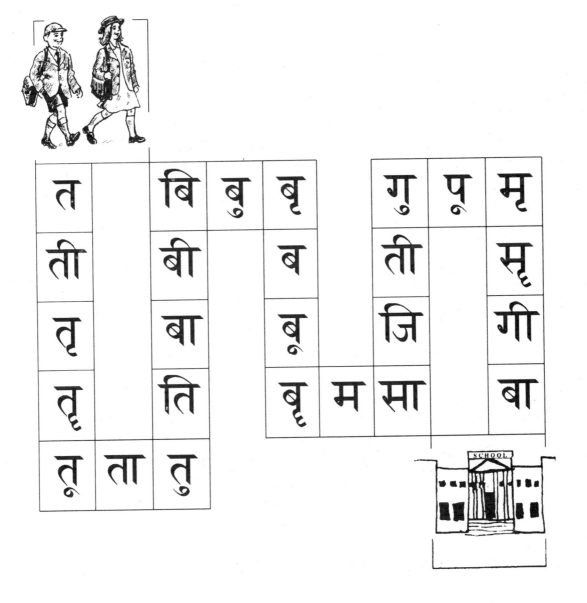

Reading Practice

Read the following across:

त	तद	तदा	
क	कद	कदा	
ऋ	ऋष	ऋषि	ऋषिः
व	वी	वीर	वीरः
न	नद	नदी	
ब	बह	बहु	
द	दू	दूत	दूतः
श	शृ	शृण	शृणु

Reading and Writing Practice

Read the following words and then copy them:

तदा	....
कदा	....
ऋषिः	....
वीरः	....
नदी	....
बहु	....
दूतः	....
शृणु	....

Alphabet Revision

Read each line across:

अ क ख ग च ङ ह

ङ ख ग ह च अ क

इ च छ ज झ ञ य श

झ छ य च ज श ञ इ

ऋ ट ठ ड ढ ण र ष

ण ऋ र ठ ष ढ ट ड

ल त य द ध न ल स

स द ल य ल त न ध

उ प फ ब भ म व

उ ब व म भ प फ

Here is how you write the letter ए.
Copy on the dotted lines.

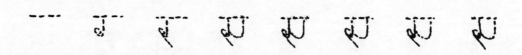

Now practice ए.

Magic Flags

One flag says **ए** as in हे हे.

When you add **ए** to a letter you add one magic flag to the top of that letter.
Read and copy the following:

ए	के	ए	ते
ए	के	ए	ते
ए	से	ए	मे
.... ____	.... ____	.... ____	.... ____
ए	ने	ए	हे
.... ____	.... ____	.... ____	.... ____

Now you add ए to the following letters.
The first one is done for you.

क	के
ज	....
श	....
द	....
न	....
ब	....
म	....
व	....

Balloon Game

Read the balloons. Then, find the other end of its string and write in the same letter in the empty balloon.

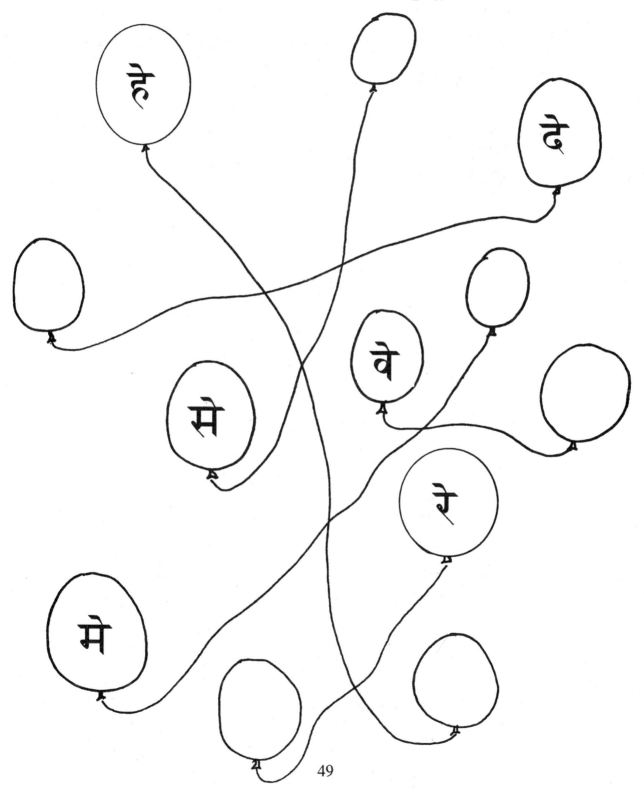

49

ऐ is very similar to ए. Sound and copy the following:

One flag says ए as in हे हे.
Two flags say ऐ as in है है.

When we add ऐ to a letter we put two
flags on the top of that letter.   Read
and copy the following:

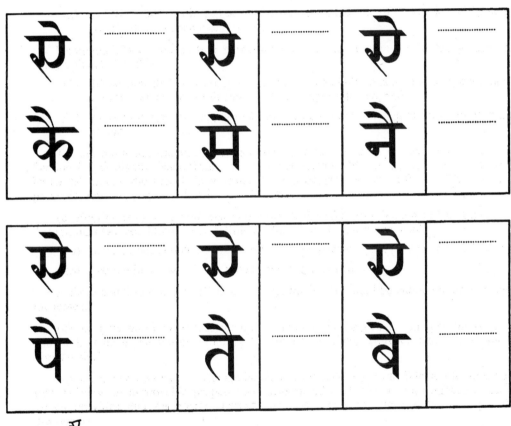

Now you add ऐ to the following letters. The first one is done for you.

क	कै
ज	
श	
द	
न	
ब	
म	
व	

The Kite Game

Read each kite. Follow its string and write in the same letter on the empty kite.

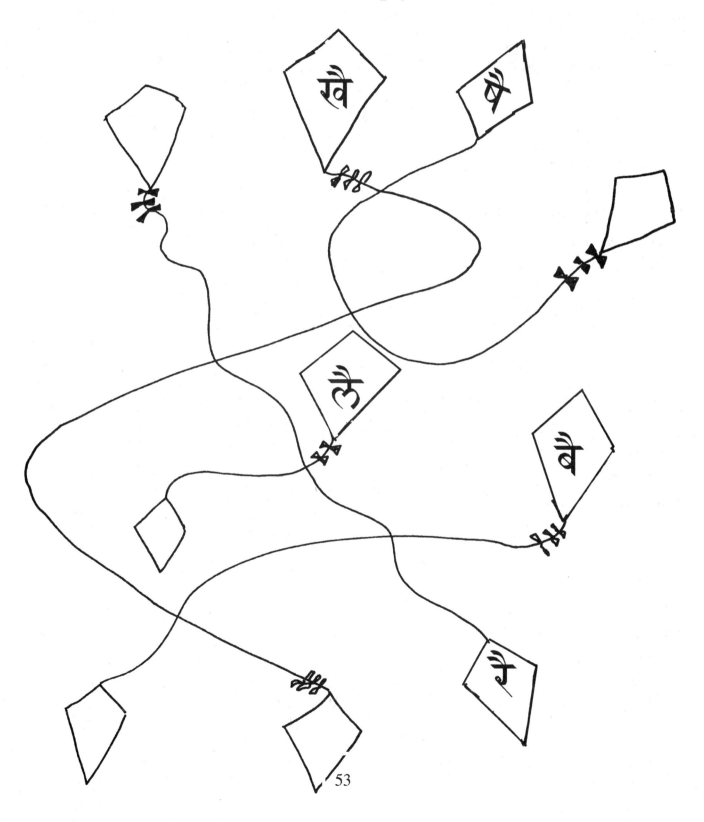

Read and copy each letter:

ए	ते	ऐ	तै
....	....	....	....
ए	चे	ऐ	चै
....	....	....	....
ए	मे	ऐ	मै
....	....	....	....

ए and ऐ

Add an ए and an ऐ to the following letters.
The first one is done for you.

क	के	कै
ग	....	....
ब	....	....
ल	....	....
प	....	....
न	....	....

ए and ऐ

Read the crocodiles' eggs.

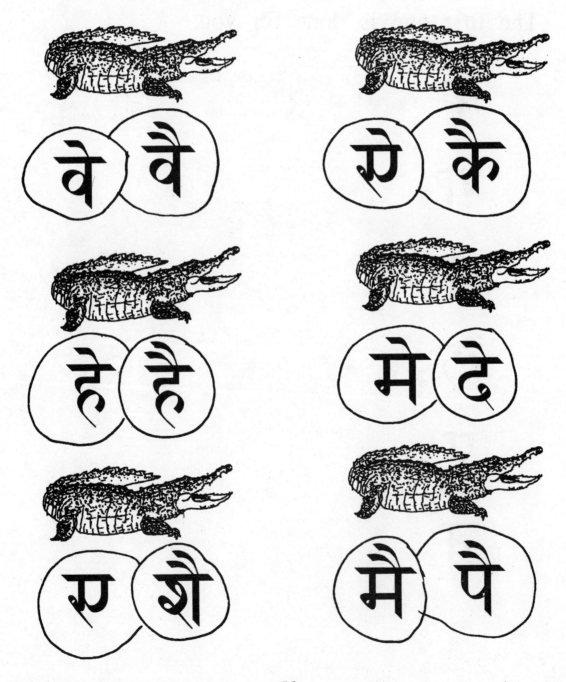

Reading Practice

Read the following words across:

क   के   केश   केशः

म   मे   मेच   मेचः

र   रा   राम   रामैः

ख   खग   खगै   खगैः

क   कप   कपे

म   सी   सीता   सीताय   सीतायै

57

Reading and Writing Practice

Read the following words and then copy them:

केशः	....
मेघः	....
रामैः	....
खगैः	....
कपे	....
सीतायै	....

ओ

Sound and copy the following:

ओ   ओ

59

One flag says ए as in हे हे.
Two flags say ऐ as in है है.
One line one flag say ओ — हो हो.

ओ

When you add ओ to a letter, you add one line and one magic flag to that letter.   Sound and write:

ओ को   ओ तो

ओ की   ओ ती

ओ लो   ओ हो

---------   ---------

ओ पो   ओ दो

---------   ---------

Now you add ओ to the following letters.
The first one is done for you.

क	को
ज	⋯⋯⋯⋯
श	⋯⋯⋯⋯
द	⋯⋯⋯⋯
न	⋯⋯⋯⋯
ब	⋯⋯⋯⋯
म	⋯⋯⋯⋯
व	⋯⋯⋯⋯

Shooting Stars

Read a star. Then find the other end.
Follow its trail of stardust to the other
star. Then fill in the same letter.

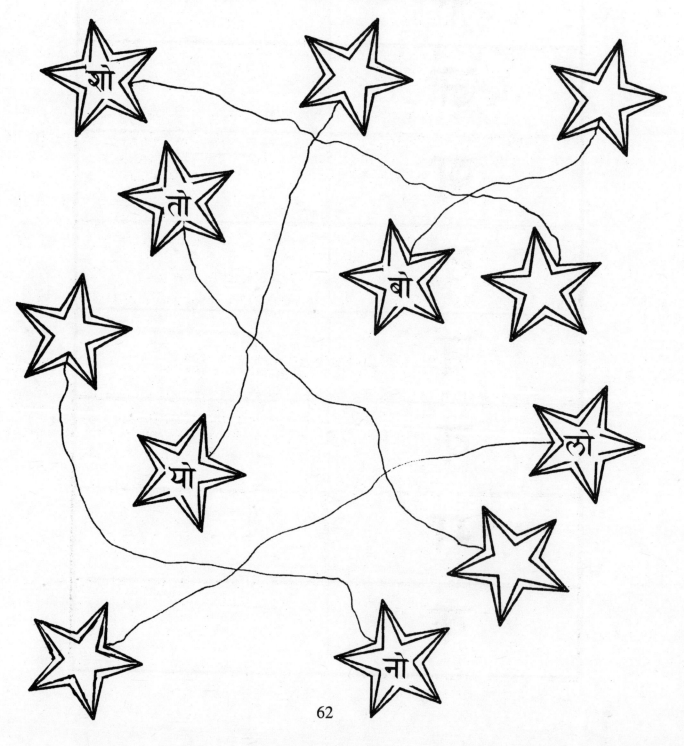

Add an ए, an ऐ, and an ओ to the following letters. The first one is done for you.

क　के　कै　को

ग

ब

श

प

न

Sound and copy the following:

One flag says ए as in हे हे.
Two flags say ऐ as in है है.
One line one flag say ओ — हो हो.
One line two flags say औ — हौ हौ.

औ

When you add औ to a letter, you add one line and two magic flags to that letter.   Sound and write.

औ	औ	औ
कौ	नौ	गौ
औ	औ	औ
पौ	चौ	मौ

Now you add an औ to the following letters.
The first one is done for you.

क	कौ
ज	....
श	....
द	....
न	....
ब	....
म	....
व	....

ओ and औ

Read the bicycles:

Find the Fish

Read each fish. Then follow the line to its pair. Now write the same letter there.

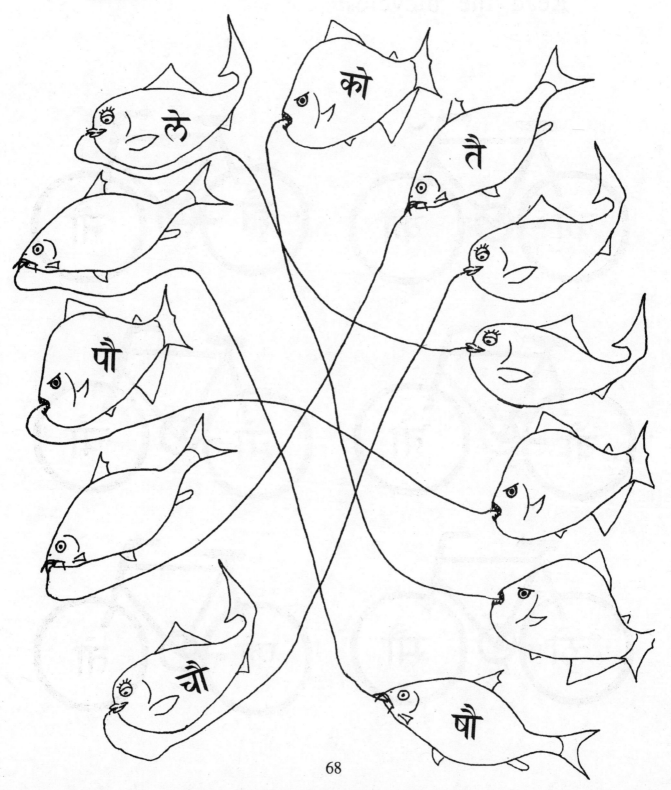

Daily Reading Chart 9

अ आ इ ई उ ऊ ऋ ॠ ऌ

ए ऐ ओ औ

अ क ख ग च ङ ह

इ च छ ज झ ञ य श

ऋ ट ठ ड ढ ण र ष

ऌ त थ द ध न ल स

उ प फ ब भ म व

ए ऐ ओ औ

Read and copy:

गे		बे		ने		जे	
गै		बै		नै		जै	
गो		बो		नो		जो	
गौ		बौ		नौ		जौ	

ए ऐ ओ औ

Add ए, ऐ, ओ and औ to the following letters.
The first one is done for you.

क	के	कै	को	कौ
ग				
द				
ष				
ह				
ण				
च				

The Vowel Giraffe

Read from the giraffe's tail up to his mouth and back again.

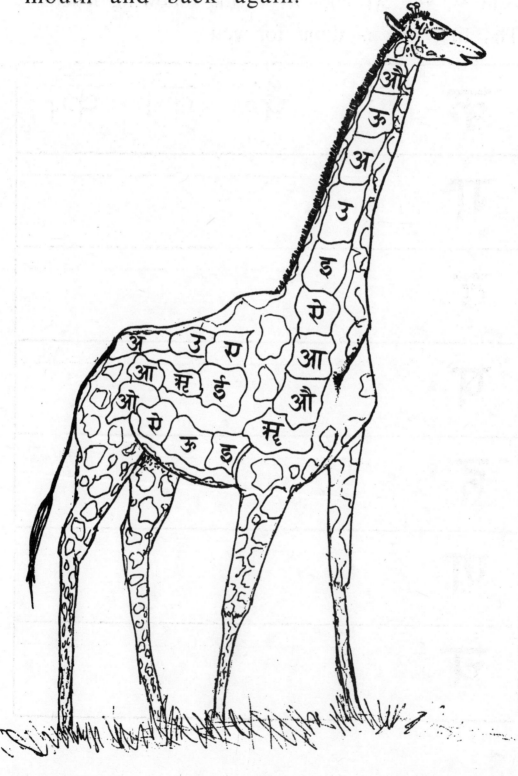

Reading Practice

Read across or down:

क	य	र	ता	हा	वा
कि	दि	मि	ति	चि	षि
कु	पु	शु	तू	लू	बू
कृ	जृ	नृ	तृ	गृ	पृ
के	फे	णे	तै	भै	मै
को	चो	डो	तौ	भौ	टौ
ता	तौ	ति	तृ	ते	तू
तै	तु	ती	तृ	तो	त

73

Reading Practice

Read the following across:

प	पे	पेट	पेटा	
र	रा	राम	रामे	रामेण
म	मो	सोद	सोदर	सोदरः
च	चो	चोर		
त	तै	तैः		
र	रा	राम	रामै	रामैः
र	रा	राम	रामौ	
ए	एक	एकद	एकदा	

Reading and Writing Practice

Read the following words and then copy them:

पेटा	....
रामेण	....
मोदरः	....
चोर	....
तैः	....
रामैः	....
रामौ	....
एकदा	....

Map Reading

	1	2	3	4	5
1	अ	य	नि	ढ	मी
2	ज	बू	फ	र	दौ
3	चु	ई	या	गी	भ
4	उ	ञ	च	शि	ट
5	छ	ॠ	ॡ	ख	ङ
6	झ	व	षे	हा	ऌ
7	गु	शृ	ध	ओ	ठ
8	ऊ	औ	इ	ड	तो
9	मा	ण	ऐ	दै	मृ

76